SO-BII-039

Orders: Please contact How2Become Ltd, Suite 14, 50 Churchill Square Business Centre, Kings Hill, Kent ME19 4YU.

You can order through Amazon.co.uk under ISBN 9781910602379, via the website www.How2Become.com or through Gardners.com.

ISBN: 9781910602379

First published in 2015 by How2Become Ltd.

Typeset for How2Become Ltd by Anton Pshinka.

Disclaimer

CONTENTS

INTRODUCTION TO YOUR GUIDE 6

GENERAL TIPS FOR VERBAL REASONING 8

EXAMPLE QUESTIONS FOR VERBAL REASONING 10

VERBAL REASONING (SECTION 1) 19

VERBAL REASONING (SECTION 2) 31

VERBAL REASONING (SECTION 3) 44

VERBAL REASONING (SECTION 4) 58

VERBAL REASONING (SECTION 5) 72

ANSWERING YOUR **QUESTIONS** 85

THE
REVISION
SERIES

INTRODUCTION TO YOUR GUIDE

Welcome to your new booklet, the *11+ Kent Test, Verbal Reasoning.* This booklet has been designed with the sole intention of aiding anyone who is taking their Kent Test, by improving their performance during the Verbal Reasoning section of the assessment.

This booklet primarily focuses on the Verbal Reasoning section of the Kent Test. It has been written to provide you with preparation tips and practice questions, which will guide you through the process of passing your Verbal Reasoning assessment.

If you wish to successfully pass all of the stages of the assessment, we highly recommend that you take a look at our other booklets for English, Maths and Non-Verbal Reasoning.

We wish you the best of luck in your assessment.

GENERAL TIPS FOR VERBAL REASONING

GENERAL TIPS FOR VERBAL REASONING

1. Some people like to work on the questions they find most difficult first. Some people prefer to leave the harder questions to last. Pick a way that you feel comfortable with, and use it throughout your Verbal Reasoning test.

2. Accuracy is key. You need to remain as accurate as possible to ensure successful marks. That's why it is important to fully comprehend the questions and understand what is being asked.

3. Make sure that you undergo practice questions under timed conditions. This will help to improve your overall performance by allowing you to practice under similar conditions to that of the real test.

4. Make sure you read the question very carefully. Some questions are designed to trick you, so you need to fully understand what the question is asking you to do, before you answer it. We recommend that you read the question at least twice before attempting to answer it.

5. Practise as many different *types* of verbal reasoning questions as you can. Within this guide we have provided you with several different question types, in order to increase your understanding and enhance your performance. Please note, the question types within this guide are not exhaustive, they are merely a way to indicate the most common types of questions found in an 11+ assessment.

6. Practise a variety of difficulty levels. If you are undergoing practice questions and are finding them relatively easy, why not practice more difficult questions? This will allow you to boost your confidence and enhance your skills. If you practise a variety of difficulty levels, you will be ready to tackle any type of Verbal Reasoning question that you encounter during the assessment.

7. Check out our free online psychometric tests and sample questions to ensure you are fully prepared for your Verbal Reasoning tests.

www.PsychometricTestsOnline.co.uk

THE
REVISION
SERIES

EXAMPLE QUESTIONS FOR VERBAL REASONING

CORRECT LETTERS

The same letter must be able to fit into both sets of brackets [?] in order to complete the word in front of the bracket, and begin the word after the bracket.

Question

Happ [?] ellow
Wh   [?] awn

A	B	C	D
W	H	Y	N

- The only letter that could fit inside the bracket in order to make 4 words is = Y.
- Happ**y**, **y**ellow, wh**y**, **y**awn

Answer

C = Y

ODD ONE OUT

Identify which word is the odd one out.

Question
A – Desk
B – Shelf
C – Cupboard
D – Chair
E – Wood

How to work it out
* The odd one out is 'wood'.
* All of the other words are objects commonly made from wood. So wood is the word linking these words together.

Answer
E – Wood

WORD JUMBLES

In the sentence, the word outside the brackets will only go with three of the words inside the brackets, in order to make a longer word. Which **ONE** *word will it* **NOT** *go with?*

Question

	A	B	C	D
Un	(adaptable	able	appropriate	afraid)

How to work it out
* Unadaptable
* Unable
* Unafraid
* **Unappropriate** is not a word. The correct term would be 'inappropriate'.

Answer
C – Appropriate

CONNECT THE WORDS

In each question, there are two pairs of words. Only one of the answers will go equally well with both of these pairs.

(Look out for meanings of the words and other possibilities of how another word could be used in that situation).

Question

(fall tumble)   (journey outing)

A	B	C	D
Travel	Trip	Trap	Drop

- 'Travel' would not be appropriate because it doesn't fit with the first set of words.
- 'Trap' doesn't work because it doesn't fit with the second set of words.
- 'Drop' doesn't work because it doesn't fit with the second set of words.

Answer

B = trip (meaning to fall or stumble) or (taking a trip somewhere).

COMPLETE THE SENTENCE

Complete the following sentence by adding in the correct words in the missing spaces.

Question

Which word makes the best sense in the following sentence?

The mechanic worked on the car for 3 hours. At the end of the 3 hours he was _____ .

A	B	C	D
home	rich	exhausted	thinking

- The only word that makes sense would be 'exhausted'.

Answer

C = exhausted

WORD FAMILIES

In each question, there are four or five words, your job is to pick out the word that links all the other words together.

EXAMPLE:

A	B	C	D
Trousers	Clothing	Shirt	Skirt

How to work it out:

- You need to work out which word can group all of the other words to form a word family.

For the above example, 'clothing' is the word that links trousers, skirt and shirt, so therefore the correct answer would be B.

Answer

B = clothing

ANTONYMS / SYNONYMS

Work out what word means the opposite or the same as the word stated.

EXAMPLE:

Beautiful

How to work out the antonym:

- Antonym means opposite, so you need to find a word that means the opposite to beautiful. For example, ugly.

How to work out the synonym:

- To work out the synonym for the above example, you need to find a word that means 'the same as'. For example, stunning.

COMPOUND WORDS

In each of the following questions, find the two words, one from each group, that together make a new, real word. The word from the group on the left always comes first.

(man bend sauce)   (tomato pan den)

How to work it out:

- In order to work out these types of questions, you need to find a word from the left group to start off the new word.

- Eliminate the answers you know to be incorrect.

- You should realise, that 'sauce' and 'pan' can be put together to make the new word 'saucepan'.

Answer

Saucepan

ALPHABET PATTERNS

In each of the following questions, find the letters that best complete the series. The alphabet has been provided to assist you.

A B C D E F G H I J K L M N O P Q R S T U V W X Y Z

PW   [ ]   XO   BK   FG   JC

A – TS
B – ST
C – RS
D – TU

How to work it out:

- Let's take the first letter of each group and work out how it is progressing. Let's start with the third group (XO) because you need to work out a common pattern.

- You should notice that the first letter is moving up the alphabet four places (4 spaces from 'x' = 'b'). Once the pattern reaches the end, it begins back at the start of the alphabet.

- So to work out the first letter of the second group, take the first group and its starting letter 'p', and add four spaces (P + 4 = T).

- Now work out how the second letter is progressing.

- You should notice that the sequence is moving down the alphabet 4 spaces. (O = K = G = C).

- So the second group needs to go down from W, 4 spaces = S.

- So therefore the correct answer is TS.

Answer

A = TS

HIDDEN WORDS

A word is hidden amongst the sentence. It has four letters and is hidden at the end of one word and the beginning of the next word. What is the hidden word?

EXAMPLE:

I need ice cold drinks during the summer time.

How to work it out:

- You need to find the hidden four letter word that is part of the ending of one word, and the beginning of the next.

- For this example, you need to pay attention to 'need' and 'ice'.

'nee**D ICE**'

Answer

Dice

VERBAL REASONING
(SECTION 1)

Question 1

What word pair shown has the most similar relationship to...

Colour : Spectrum

A	B	C	D
Verse : Rhyme	Waves : Sound	Tone : Scale	Nature : Atmosphere

Question 2

Which **one** word has a meaning that extends to, or includes, the meaning of all the other words?

A	B	C	D	E
Gymnastics	Swimming	Running	Training	Football

Question 3

A word is hidden amongst the sentence. It has four letters and is hidden at the end of one word and is the beginning of the next word. What word is hidden?

For the last time, I will not tell you again.

Answer [   ]

Question 4

Which word does not have a similar meaning to – imaginary?

A	B	C	D
Mythical	Fictional	Illusive	Fickle

Question 5

In the line below, the word outside of the brackets will only go with three of the words inside the brackets to make longer words. Which ONE word will it NOT go with?

	A	B	C	D
Un	(affected	alike	adjusted	capable)

Answer [ ]

Question 6

Which of the following words is the odd one out?

A	B	C
Forever	New	Fresh

Question 7

Which word is the odd one out?

A	B	C	D	E
Ostrich	Parrots	Penguins	Dodo	Owls

Question 8

In the line below, the word outside of the brackets will only go with three of the words inside the brackets to make longer words. Which **one** word will it **not** go with?

	A	B	C	D
Un	(assuming	admired	usual	draught)

Answer [ ]

Question 9

Four of the five sentences have the same meaning. Which **one** sentence has a **different** meaning?

A – Mike spent £180 during his shopping trip.

B – During his shopping trip, Mike spent £180.

C – The shopping trip cost Mike £180.

D – Mike made £180 from his shopping trip.

E – A total of £180 was spent on Mike's shopping trip.

Answer

Question 10

In the line below, the word outside of the brackets will only go with three of the words inside the brackets to make longer words. Which **one** word will it **not** go with?

	A	B	C	D
An	(tarctic	aerobic	ability	droid)

Answer

Question 11

Fill in the missing words so that the sentence reads correctly.

He _____ the telephone and then _____ it to his mother.

A	B	C	D
heard / shouted	answered / spoke	picked / threw	answered / passed

Question 12

Fill in the missing word so that the sentence reads correctly.

‑‑‑‑‑‑‑‑‑ going to be in big trouble when they get home.

A	B	C	D
Thair	There	Their	They're

Question 13

In the line below, the word outside of the brackets will only go with three of the words inside the brackets to make longer words. Which **one** word will it **not** go with?

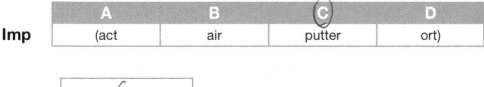

	A	B	C	D
Imp	(act	air	putter	ort)

Answer

Question 14

Which of the following is the odd one out?

A	B	C	D
Trumpet	Violin	Harp	Guitar

Question 15

The following sentence has one word missing. Which **one** word makes the best sense when placed in the sentence?

A submarine is a vehicle that is ‑‑‑‑‑‑‑‑‑ of independent operation underwater.

A	B	C	D	E
evolved	built	capable	designed	submersible

Question 16

Four of the five sentences have the same meaning. Which **one** sentence has a **different** meaning?

A – It was a little girl who was pushed over by the tall boy.

B – The tall boy pushed over a little girl.

C – The little girl pushed over the boy.

D – The little girl fell over as a result of being pushed by the tall boy.

E – The tall boy got into trouble for pushing over a little girl.

Answer

Question 17

In the line below, the word outside of the brackets will only go with three of the words inside the brackets to make longer words. Which **one** word will it **not** go with?

	A	B	C	D
Im	(age	agine	moral	signficant)

Answer

Question 18

The following sentence has one word missing. Which **one** word makes the best sense when placed in the sentence?

The man _____ he wanted to go home.

A	B	C	D	E
chose	needed	decided	ran	boasted

Question 19

The following sentence has **one** word missing. Which **one** word makes the best sense when placed in the sentence?

The weather forecaster informed the public of the _____ rain.

A	B	C	D	E
likelihood	chance	dry	need	potential

Question 20

Which of the following words is the odd one out?

A	B	C	D
Circle	Rectangle	Sphere	Triangle

Question 21

Which letter is missing from the following words?

HER (_) RAG and **BLUR (_) ALL**

A	B	C	D
B	S	T	U

Question 22

Which of the following is the odd one out?

A	B	C	D	E
Rose	Lily	Daisy	Petal	Sunflower

Question 23

Which letter is missing from the following words?

FEE (_) ARE and **PLEA (_) ATE**

A	B	C	D
D	L	S	Y

Question 24

Which of the following is the odd one out?

A	B	C	D
Now	Cow	Low	How

Question 25

In the line below, the word outside of the brackets will only go with three o
the words inside the brackets to make longer words. Which ONE word will i
NOT go with?

	A	B	C	D
In	(decisive	reference	destructible	convenience)

Answer

ANSWERS TO SECTION 1

Q1. C = Tone : Scale

EXPLANATION = for this type of question, you need to work out what two words have the most similar meaning to the two words shown. 'Colour' and 'spectrum' both can be related to 'tone' and 'scale'. Colours have different tones and can be defined on a scale i.e. light and dark; just like a spectrum has a scale and tones of colours.

Q2. D = training

EXPLANATION = 'training' is the one word that groups all of the other words together. *Gymnastics, swimming, running* and *football* are all types of *training* exercises for an athletic sport.

Q3. Fort

EXPLANATION = '**for the**'.

Q4. D = fickle

EXPLANATION = *fictional, illusive* and *mythical* are all words that relate to 'imaginary'. *Fickle* does not carry the same connotations as these words and therefore does not have a similar meaning.

Q5. D = capable

EXPLANATION = if you were to put 'un' with the words 'affected', 'alike' and 'adjusted', you would get: *unaffected, unalike* and *unadjusted*. However, if you tried to put 'un' with 'capable', it would not be grammatically correct. Therefore answer D does not go with the word outside of the bracket.

Q6. A = forever

EXPLANATION = 'forever' is the odd one out because both 'new' and 'fresh' have a similar meaning.

Q7. D = dodo

EXPLANATION = all of the other words refer to birds that are not extinct.

Q8. D = draught

EXPLANATION = if you were to put 'un' with the words 'assuming, 'admired', and 'usual', you would get: *unassuming, unadmired* and *unusual*. However, if you were to put 'un' with 'draught', this would not be grammatically correct.

Q9. D = Mike made £180 from his shopping trip

EXPLANATION = the other four sentences refer to Mike spending money, therefore answer option D (Mike made £180 from his shopping trip) means something different.

Q10. C = ability

EXPLANATION = if were to put 'an' with 'tarctic', 'aerobic' and 'droid', you would get: *Antarctic, anaerobic* and *android*. However, if you were to put 'an' with 'ability', this would not be grammatically correct.

Q11. D = answered / passed

EXPLANATION = He **answered** the telephone and then **passed** it to his mother.

Q12. D = they're

EXPLANATION = in order to find the missing word, you need to work out the sentence structure. Is it in past tense, present tense or future tense? The word that is grammatically correct for this sentence is 'they're'. So, the sentence would read 'they're (they are) going to be in big trouble when they get home'.

Q13. C = putter

EXPLANATION = *impact, impair, import.* Therefore the word that does not fit with (imp) is 'putter'. *'Impputter'* is not a word, and therefore does not fit with the word outside of the brackets.

Q14. A = trumpet

EXPLANATION = trumpet is the only instrument listed that requires you to play using your mouth. The other instruments require you to play the instrument using your hands.

Q15. C = capable

EXPLANATION = the word that would best fit the sentence is 'capable'. So, the sentence would read: 'a submarine is a watercraft **capable** of independent operation underwater'.

Q16. C = the little girl pushed over the boy.

EXPLANATION = the sentence 'the little girl pushed over the boy' has the opposite meaning to all of the other sentences, therefore this sentence is the odd one out.

Q17. D = significant

EXPLANATION = if you were to put 'im' with 'age', 'agine' and 'moral', you would get: *image, imagine* and *immoral*. However, if you were to put 'im' with 'significant', this would be grammatically incorrect.

Q18. C = decided

EXPLANATION = the correct word is 'decided'. So, the sentence would read 'the man **decided** he wanted to go home'.

Q19. E = potential

EXPLANATION = the word that is needed in order to make the sentence grammatically correct is 'potential'. So, the sentence would read 'the weather forecaster informed the public of the **potential** rain'.

Q20. C = sphere

EXPLANATION = 'sphere' is the odd one out because all of the other words refer to 2D shapes. A sphere is 3-dimensional.

Q21. A = B

EXPLANATION = *herb, brag, blurb* and *ball*.

Q22. D = petal

EXPLANATION = 'petal' is the odd one out because all of the other words refer to 'types' of flowers, whereas a petal is 'part' of a flower.

Q23. A = D

EXPLANATION = *feed, dare, plead* and *date*.

Q24. C = low

EXPLANATION = 'low' is the odd one out, because it is pronounced differently from the other three words.

Q25. B = reference

EXPLANATION = if you were to put the word 'in' with the words 'decisive' 'destructible' and 'convenience', you would get: *indecisive, indestructible* and *inconvenience*. However, if you were to put the word 'in' with the word 'reference', this would be grammatically incorrect.

VERBAL REASONING
(SECTION 2)

Question 1

Which of the following words is the odd one out?

A	B	C	D	E
Swim	Run	Sprint	Sit	Walk

Question 2

Choose one letter that can be moved from the word on the left to the word on the right, making two new words.

DRINK   FREE

A	B	C	D	E
D	R	I	N	K

Question 3

Choose one letter that can be moved from the word on the left to the word on the right, making two new words.

RULER   STAY

A	B	C	D
R	U	L	E

Question 4

Which five letter word can be placed in **front** of the following words to make a new word?

making   wood   stick   box

Answer [   ]

Question 5

The sentence below has a word missing. Which one word makes the best sense when placed in the sentence?

The news reporter had very little time to _____ his interview with the famous actor.

A	B	C	D
conduct	fix	make	reach

Question 6

Which of the following is the odd one out?

A	B	C	D
July	December	June	May

Question 7

Which of the following sentences has a different meaning to the other four sentences?

A – On the floor was a man, who was pushed over by the bouncer.

B – The bouncer pushed a man to the floor.

C – The man was pushed to the floor by a bouncer.

D – The man was pushed by the bouncer onto the floor.

E – The bouncer was pushed by a man, who then fell to the floor.

Answer [   ]

Question 8

In each question, there are two pairs of words. Only one of the answers wi
go equally well with both these pairs.

(Dog   Woof)   (Tree   Wood)

A	B	C	D
Animal	Bark	Sycamore	Tail

Question 9

Which of the following words is the odd one out?

A	B	C	D
Dragon	Dog	Dolphin	Donkey

Question 10

Which of the following is the odd one out?

A	B	C	D	E
Sight	Height	Eight	Night	Flight

Question 11

Which of the following is the odd one out?

A	B	C	D	E
Lonely	Solitary	Secluded	Sheltered	Affable

Question 12

In the line below, the word outside of the brackets will only go with three of the words inside the brackets to make longer words. Which **one** word will it **not** go with?

	A	B	C	D
Un	(interested	able	anticipated	different)

Answer

Question 13

Which four letter word can be placed in **front** of the following words, in order to make four new words?

where   **thing**   **one**   **time**

Answer

Question 14

The following sentence has one word missing. Which of the following words makes best sense when placed in the sentence?

I can't _____ what their family must be going through.

A – think

B – imagine

C – anything

D – help

E – like

Answer

Question 15

Which of the following words is the odd one out?

A	B	C	D	E
First	Second	Third	Forth	Fifth

Question 16

The following sentence has one word missing. Which word makes the best sense when placed in the sentence?

She wanted a new dress for her birthday but _ _ _ _ _ _ _ she received some pyjamas.

A – hoped

B – again

C – replace

D – instead

E – now

Answer

Question 17

The following sentence has one word missing. Which word makes the best sense when placed in the sentence?

The class was asked to write a poem that _ _ _ _ _ _ _ _ _ .

A – rimed

B – ryhmed

C – rhymed

D – rymed

Answer

Question 18

Which of the following words is the odd one out?

A	B	C	D	E
Blue	Green	Violet	Black	Orange

Question 19

In the line below, the word outside of the brackets will only go with three of the words inside the brackets to make longer words. Which **one** word will it **not** go with?

	A	B	C	D
Dis	(familiar	regard	belief	able)

Answer

Question 20

Which of the following words is the odd one out?

A	B	C	D	E
Ducks	Trees	Water	People	Books

Question 21

The following sentence has two words missing. Which two words make best sense when placed in the sentence?

It was _____ responsibility and they had to _____ the consequences.

A – there / face

B – their / see

C – their / choose

D – their / face

E – they're / find

Answer

Question 22

Which of the following words is the odd one out?

A	B	C	D	E
Television	Microwave	Camera	Hairdryer	Cooker

Question 23

Which of the following words is the odd one out?

A	B	C	D	E
Frown	Down	Gown	Shown	Town

Question 24

The following sentence has two words missing. Which words makes the best sense when placed in the sentence?

Sometimes you have to make choices, _____ _____ they may not always be the correct ones.

A	B	C	D	E
even though	although they	even although	despite being	if even

Question 25

Which of the following words is the odd one out?

A	B	C	D	E
Oak	Fir	Wood	Ash	Beech

ANSWERS TO SECTION 2

Q1. D = sit

EXPLANATION = the word 'sit' is the odd one out because all of the other words refer to types of exercise.

Q2. A = d

EXPLANATION = if you move the 'd' from 'drink', you would get 'rink. If you put the 'd' in the word 'free', you would get 'freed'.

Q3. A = r

EXPLANATION = if you removed the 'r' from the word 'ruler', you would get 'rule'. If you put the 'r' with the word 'stay', you would get 'stray'.

Q4. Match

EXPLANATION = *matchmaking, matchwood, matchstick* and *matchbox*.

Q5. A = conduct

EXPLANATION = in order to find the best word to complete the sequence, you need to understand the structure of the sentence. In this sentence, the best word that would fit with the structure of the sentence is 'conduct'. So, the sentence would read: 'the news reporter had very little time to **conduct** his interview with the famous actor'.

Q6. B = December

EXPLANATION = 'December' is the odd one out because all of the other words are months that are in spring/summer time, whereas December is in the winter.

Q7. E = The bouncer was pushed by a man, who then fell to the floor

EXPLANATION = all of the other sentences refer to the bouncer pushing a man to the floor. However the sentence 'the bouncer was pushed by a man who then fell to the floor' has a different meaning to all of the other sentences.

Q8. B = bark

EXPLANATION = 'bark' can refer to a 'dog' and the sound that a dog makes i.e. 'woof' or 'bark', or it can refer to a part of a 'tree', made from 'wood'.

Q9. A = dragon

EXPLANATION = 'dragon' is the odd one out, because all of the other animals are real, whereas a dragon is a mythological creature.

Q10. C = eight

EXPLANATION = 'eight' is the odd one out because all of the other the words end in 'ight'. 'Eight' is pronounced differently.

Q11. E = affable

EXPLANATION = 'affable' is the odd one out because all of the other words are synonyms of being lonely, whereas 'affable' refers to being sociable and friendly.

Q12. D = different

EXPLANATION = if you were to put 'un' with the words 'interested', 'able', and 'anticipated', you would get: *uninterested, unable* and *unanticipated*. However, if you were to put 'un' with 'different', this would not be grammatically correct.

Q13. Some

EXPLANATION = *some*where, *some*thing, *some*one and *some*time.

Q14. B = imagine

EXPLANATION = the word that would best complete the sequence would be 'imagine'. So the sentence would read: *'I can't **imagine** what their family must be going through'*. This makes the most sense.

Q15. D = forth

EXPLANATION = 'forth' is the odd one out because it is spelt incorrectly. I the sequence, it refers to numbers, so therefore it should be 'fourth' not 'forth' 'Forth' is a word used to describe moving onwards in time, i.e. forwards c away.

Q16. D = instead

EXPLANATION = the correct word that can be used in order to complete th sentence is 'instead'. The sentence would read as follows: *'She wanted a new dress for her birthday but instead she received some pyjamas'.*

Q17. C = rhymed

EXPLANATION = the word that would best complete the sequence would b 'rhymed'. This is the only correct spelling of the word: *'The class was asked to write a poem that rhymed'.*

Q18. D = black

EXPLANATION = 'black' is the odd one out because all of the other colour are colours that form a rainbow.

Q19. A = familiar

EXPLANATION = if you were to put 'dis' with the words 'regard', 'belief', an 'able', you would get: *disregard, disbelief* and *disable*. However, if you were t put 'dis' with 'familiar', this would not be grammatically correct.

Q20. C = water

EXPLANATION = 'water' is the odd one out because this word is a uncountable noun; all of the other words can be counted i.e. number c ducks, number of trees etc.

Q21. D = their / face

EXPLANATION = the sentence would best read as follows: *'It was **their** responsibility and they had to **face** the consequences.'*

Q22. C = camera

EXPLANATION = 'camera' is the odd one out because all of the other words refer to a household appliance.

Q23. D = shown

EXPLANATION = 'shown' is the odd one out because, while all of the words end in 'own', 'shown' is pronounced differently

Q24. A = even though

EXPLANATION = the sentence would best read as follows: *'Sometimes you have to make choices, **even though** they may not always be the correct ones'.*

Q25. C = wood

EXPLANATION = 'wood' is the odd one out because all of the other words refer to *types* of wood, and 'wood' is the word that links them together.

THE
REVISION
SERIES

VERBAL REASONING
(SECTION 3)

Question 1

The following sentence has two words missing. Which words make the best sense when placed in the sentence?

The train service has _____ customers that there may be several delays because of _____ difficulties.

A – informed / financial

B – said / rail

C – stated / track

D – requested / electrical

E – informed / technical

Answer ┌────────────┐
       │   E   │
       └────────────┘

Question 2

Which of the following words is the odd one out?

A	B	C	D	E
Treasure	Grass	Ship	Skull	Map

Question 3

Which four letter word can be placed at the **end** of the following words, in order to create four new words?

King   Parent   Adult   Liveli

Answer ┌────────────┐
       │   hood   │
       └────────────┘

Question 4

Which four letter word can be placed at the **end** of the following words, in order to create four new words?

Accept   *Charit*   *Foresee*   *Float*

Answer [   ]

Question 5

The following sentence has one word missing. Which **one** word makes the best sense when placed in the sentence?

He needed to be .... for what he had done.

A – helped

B – reprimanded

C – stopped

D – fixed

E – custody

Answer [   ]

Question 6

Which of the following words is the odd one out?

A	B	C	D	E
Grass	Flowers	Worms	Mud	Wasp

Question 7

The following sentence has one word missing. Which one word makes the best sense when placed in the sentence?

Sarah was the manager of a company and was .... for all types of problems.

A – responsible

B – dealt with

C – possessing

D – encountered

E – subject

Answer

Question 8

Which of the following words is the odd one out?

A	B	C	D	E
Pence	Pounds	Euros	Coins	Dime

Question 9

In the line below, the word outside of the brackets will only go with three of the words inside the brackets to make longer words. Which **one** word will it **not** go with?

	A	B	C	D
Bru	(ken	shed	talities	nette)

Answer

Question 10

Which of the following words is the odd one out?

A	B	C	D	E
Cup	Fork	Knife	Teaspoon	Spoon

Question 11

The following sentence has two words missing. Which words make the best sense when placed in the sentence?

We are about to _____ upon a _____ adventure.

A – run / treacherous
B – join / treacherous
C – board / different
D – embark / treacherous
E – head / wild

Answer

Question 12

The following sentence has one word missing. Which word makes the best sense when placed in the sentence?

I find it difficult to _____ Mia's reasons as to why she is marrying him.

A – clarify
B – comprehend
C – utilise
D – state
E – illustrate

Answer

Question 13

In the line below, the word outside of the brackets will only go with three of the words inside the brackets to make longer words. Which **one** word will it **not** go with?

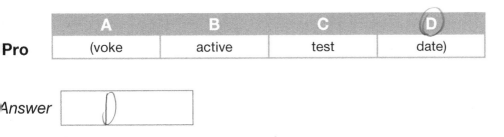

	A	B	C	D
Pro	(voke	active	test	date)

Answer ☐

Question 14

The following sentence has one word missing. Which word makes the best sense when placed in the sentence?

It was an _____ first kiss.

A – good
B – pleasing
C – uninteresting
D – unforgettable
E – undeniable

Answer ☐

Question 15

Which two words are the most opposite in meaning?

Frightened, panicked, worried, ecstatic, worried, devastated

Answer ☐

Question 16

Which two words are the most opposite in meaning?

Conclusion, decision, outcome, initiation, result, probability

Answer

Question 17

If the following words were placed in alphabetical order, which one would be third?

A	B	C	D
Delightful	Delicious	Delayed	Delicate

Answer

Question 18

Chair is to sit, as ladder is to?

A – Climb

B – Step

C – Bridge

D – Metal

E – Heavy

Answer

Question 19

If the following words were placed in alphabetical order, which one would be fourth?

A	B	C	D	E
Plausible	Plagiarise	Plastics	Plasters	Plaque

Question 20

Choose one letter that can be moved from the word on the left to the word on the right, making two new words.

CLOCK   **RANK**

A – C

B – L

C – O

D – K

Answer [   ]

Question 21

Choose one letter that can be moved from the word on the left to the word on the right, making two new words.

REED   **BAR**

A – R

B – E

C – D

Answer [   ]

Question 22

Choose one letter that can be moved from the word on the left to the word on the right, making two new words.

VOICE   *SCAR*

A – V

B – O

C – I

D – C

E – E

Answer

Question 23

Which word is the odd one out?

A – Bark

B – Sun

C – Tree

Answer

Question 24

Which letter is missing from the following words?

Taugh[?]   [?]hing   tigh[?]   [?]ile

A – T

B – S

C – E

D – N

Answer

Question 25

Which letter is missing from the following words?

Skate[?]   [?]ace   clove[?]   [?]after

A – E

B – S

C – P

D – R

Answer

ANSWERS TO SECTION 3

Q1. E = informed / technical

EXPLANATION = the sentence would best read as follows: *'The train servic* *has* **informed** *customers that there may be several delays because c* **technical** *difficulties'.*

Q2. B = grass

EXPLANATION = 'grass' is the odd one out because all of the other word refer to pirates, whereas 'grass' has no clear relationship with any of th words.

Q3. hood

EXPLANATION = king*hood*, parent*hood*, adult*hood* and liveli*hood*.

Q4. able

EXPLANATION = accept*able,* charit*able,* foresee*able* and float*able*.

Q5. B = reprimanded

EXPLANATION = the sentence would read best as follows: *'He needed to b* **reprimanded** *for what he had done'.*

Q6. D = mud

EXPLANATION = 'mud' is the odd one out because all of the other word refer to living organisms, whereas mud is not 'alive' so to speak.

Q7. A = responsible

EXPLANATION = the sentence would best read as follows: *'Sarah was th* *manager of a company and was* **responsible** *for all types of problems'.*

Q8. D = coins

EXPLANATION = 'coins' is the odd one out because this word refers to all of the other words; the rest of the words are all *types* of coin.

Q9. A = ken

EXPLANATION = if you were to put 'bru' with the words 'shed', 'talities' and 'nette', you would get: *brushed, brutalities* and *brunette*. However, if you tried to put 'bru' with 'ken', this would be grammatically incorrect.

Q10. A = cup

EXPLANATION = 'cup' is the odd one out because all of the other words are types of cutlery, whereas a 'cup' is an item of crockery.

Q11. D = embark / treacherous

EXPLANATION = the sentence would best read as follows: *'We are about to* **embark** *upon a* **treacherous** *adventure'.*

Q12. B = comprehend

EXPLANATION = the sentence would read best as follows: *'I find it difficult to* **comprehend** *Mia's reasons as to why she is marrying him'.*

Q13. D = date

EXPLANATION = if you were to put 'pro' with the words 'voke', 'active' and 'test', you would get: *provoke, proactive* and *protest*. However, if you tried to put 'pro' with 'date', this would be grammatically incorrect.

Q14. D = unforgettable

EXPLANATION = the sentence would read best as follows: *'It was an* **unforgettable** *first kiss'.*

Q15. Ecstatic and devastated

EXPLANATION = ecstatic and devastated are the most opposite in meaning.

Q16. Initiation and conclusion

EXPLANATION = initiation and conclusion are the most opposite in meaning.

Q17. B = delicious

EXPLANATION = in alphabetical order, the words would read as follows: *delayed, delicate, delicious* and *delightful*. So the third word in the sequence would be 'delicious'.

Q18. A = climb

EXPLANATION = chair is to sit on, as ladder is to climb.

Q19. C = plastics

EXPLANATION = if you were to put the words in alphabetical, they would be: *plagiarise, plaque, plasters, plastics* and *plausible*. Therefore, the word that would come fourth after being alphabetised, is *plastics*.

Q20. A = C

EXPLANATION = if you removed the 'c' from 'clock', you would get 'lock'. If you put the 'c' in 'rank', you would get 'crank'.

Q21. B = E

EXPLANATION = if you removed the 'e' from 'reed', you would get 'red'. If you put the 'e' with 'bar', you would get 'bare'.

Q22. B = O

EXPLANATION = if you removed the 'o' from 'voice' you would get 'vice'. If you put the 'o' with 'scar', you would get 'oscar'.

Q23. B = sun

EXPLANATION = 'sun' is the odd one out because 'bark' is a part of a 'tree', so these two words are closely linked. Whereas 'sun' has no clear link to either.

Q24. A = T

EXPLANATION = *taught, thing, tight* and *tile*.

Q25. D = R

EXPLANATION = *skater, race, clover* and *rafter*.

THE
REVISION
SERIES

VERBAL REASONING
(SECTION 4)

Question 1

Insert the missing word.

If you are _____ at the written tests, you will progress to the next stage.

A – okay

B – fail

C – work

D – successful

E – pass

Answer

Question 2

If the following words were arranged in alphabetical order, which word would be second?

A	B	C	D	E
Believe	Beast	Belief	Bereaved	Best

Question 3

In the line below, the word outside of the brackets will only go with three of the words inside the brackets to make longer words. Which ONE word will it NOT go with?

Mis

A	B	C	D
(interpret	judge	handle	merise)

Answer   D

Question 4

The following sentence has one word missing. Which ONE word makes the best sense when placed in the sentence?

He had to serve eight years of his sentence before he would be ‑‑‑‑‑‑‑‑‑‑ .

A – sentenced

B – custody

C – released

D – rehabilitation

E – convict

Answer

Question 5

The following sentence has two words missing. Which TWO words make the best sense when placed in the sentence?

Marketing is a process that allows an organisation to ‑‑‑‑‑‑‑‑‑ its resources on the opportunities that will allow it to ‑‑‑‑‑‑‑‑ sales and achieve a sustainable competitive advantage.

A – concentrate / direct

B – direct / lose

C – focus / increase

D – process / increase

E – deliver / focus

Answer

Question 6

Which of the following words is the odd one out?

A	B	C	D
Bench	Stool	Chair	Sit

Question 7

Which of the following words is the odd one out?

A	B	C	D	E
Ear	Leg	Mouth	Nostril	Eye

Question 8

Which of the following words is the odd one out?

A	B	C	D	E
Water	Lake	River	Reservoir	Pool

Question 9

Which of the following words is the odd one out?

A	B	C	D	E
Car	Train	Boat	Garage	Bicycle

Question 10

Which of the following words is the odd one out?

A	B	C	D	E
Milk	Tea	Coffee	Sugar	Spoon

Question 11

In the line below, the word outside of the brackets will only go with three of the words inside the brackets to make longer words. Which ONE word will NOT go with?

	A	B	C	D
In	(decent	direct	appropriate	abusive)

Answer [D]

Question 12

The following sentence has one word missing. Which word makes the best sense when placed in the sentence?

He had spent many years in the same job and was now starting to become _____ with all of the meetings he had to attend.

A – daring

B – caring

C – irritated

D – honourable

E – frightened

Answer [C]

Question 13

Which of the following words is the odd one out?

A	B	C	D	E
Hut	Flat	Shed	House	Park

Question 14

Which of the following words is closest in meaning to - *desire*?

A – Achieve
B – Wish
C – Get
D – Determine
E – Believe

Answer B

Question 15

Which of the following words contains the most vowels?

A – Reasonable
B – Combination
C – Vegetables
D – Audaciously

Answer

Question 16

Which of the following words contains the least vowels?

A – Barber
B – Radio
C – Disastrous
D – Elephant
E – March

Answer

Question 17

Which of the following words is closest in meaning to - *gather*?

A – Assemble

B – Around

C – Stay

D – Refute

E – Disembark

Answer

Question 18

Insert the missing word:

There are two aspects to _____ good habits.

A – organising

B – unfolding

C – making

D – developing

E – start

Answer

Question 19

Insert the missing word.

After satisfactory _____ *of the medical, you will be measured for your uniform.*

A – pass

B – sample

C – attendance

D – completion

E – being

Answer

Question 20

In the line below, the word outside of the brackets will only go with three of the words inside the brackets to make longer words. Which ONE word will it NOT go with?

A	B	C	D
(infect	able	cent	advantage)

Dis

Answer

Question 21

In the line below, the word outside of the brackets will only go with three o the words inside the brackets to make longer words. Which ONE word will NOT go with?

	A	B	C	D
Pre	(dict	bable	mature	sent)

Answer [B]

Question 22

Which word is the odd one out?

A – Flight
B – Height
C – Despite
D – Sight
E – Light

Answer [ ]

Question 23

Which word contains the most vowels?

A – Importance
B – Dignity
C – Undeniable
D – Indifferent
E – Forgettable

Answer [ ]

Question 24

Which word contains the least amount of vowels?

A – Fraudulent

B – Belittled

C – Significant

D – Tailored

E – Rhythm

Answer

Question 25

Mark can run faster than Jane. Jane can run faster than Nigel who is slower than Bill. Bill runs faster than Mark. Who is the slowest?

A – Nigel

B – Mark

C – Jane

D – Bill

Answer

ANSWERS TO SECTION 4

Q1. D = successful

EXPLANATION = if you are **successful** at the written tests, you will progress to the next stage.

Q2. C = belief

EXPLANATION = in alphabetical order, the words would be written as follows: *beast, belief, believe, bereaved* and *best*. So the second word in the order is *belief*.

Q3. D = merise

EXPLANATION = if you were to put 'mis' with the words 'interpret', 'judge' and 'handle', you would get *misinterpret, misjudge* and *mishandle*, whereas 'mis' cannot be put with the word 'merise'.

Q4. C = released

EXPLANATION = he had to serve eight years of his sentence before he would be **released**.

Q5. C = focus / increase

EXPLANATION = Marketing is a process that allows an organisation to **focus** its resources on the opportunities that will allow it to **increase** sales and achieve a sustainable competitive advantage.

Q6. D = sit

EXPLANATION = 'sit' is the odd one out because all of the other words refer to types of furniture that you sit on.

Q7. B = leg

EXPLANATION = 'leg' is the odd one out because all of the other words refer to features that can be found on your face/head.

Q8. A = water

EXPLANATION = 'water' is the odd one out because all of the other words require water i.e. lakes, pools, reservoirs etc.

Q9. D = garage

EXPLANATION = 'garage' is the odd one out because all of the other words refer to types of transport.

Q10. E = spoon

EXPLANATION = 'spoon' is the odd one out because all of the other words refer to items that you need to make a cup of tea/coffee. A spoon is not an ingredient to make tea or coffee, and therefore is the odd one out.

Q11. D = abusive

EXPLANATION = if you put 'in' with the words 'decent', 'direct' and 'appropriate', you would get *indecent, indirect* and *inappropriate*. However 'in' cannot be placed with the word 'abusive'; as this would be grammatically incorrect.

Q12. C = irritated

EXPLANATION = He had spent many years in the same job and was now starting to become **irritated** with all of the meetings he had to attend.

Q13. E = park

EXPLANATION = 'park' is the odd one out because all of the other words refer to places of residence/buildings.

Q14. B = wish

EXPLANATION = desire has the closest meaning to wish. If you desire something, you wish for it.

Q15. D = audaciously

EXPLANATION = the word 'audaciously' contains six vowels. None of th other answer options contains more vowels, so therefore this is the correc answer.

Q16. E = march

EXPLANATION = the word 'march' only contains one vowel. No other answe option contains less vowels, so therefore this is the correct answer.

Q17. A = assemble

EXPLANATION = assemble is the closest in meaning to gather. Both thes words refer to collective groupings.

Q18. D = developing

EXPLANATION = There are two aspects to **developing** good habits.

Q19. D = completion

EXPLANATION = *after satisfactory* **completion** *of the medical, you will b measured for your uniform.*

Q20. C = cent

EXPLANATION = if you were to put the word 'dis' with the words 'infect', 'able and 'advantage', you would get *disinfect, disable* and *disadvantage*. Howeve if you were to put the word 'dis' with 'cent', this would be grammaticall incorrect.

Q21. B = bable

EXPLANATION = if you were to put the word 'pre' with the words 'dict 'mature' and 'sent', you would get *predict, premature* and *present*. Howeve if you were to put the word 'pre' with 'bable', this would be grammaticall incorrect.

Q22. C = despite

EXPLANATION = 'despite' is the odd one out because although the words all end in the 'ight' / 'ite' sound, 'despite' is spelt with a different ending. All of the other words end in 'ight', whereas 'despite' ends in 'ite'.

Q23. C = undeniable

EXPLANATION = 'undeniable' contains five vowels. No other answer option contains more vowels, so therefore this is the correct answer.

Q24. E = rhythm

EXPLANATION = 'rhythm' contains no vowels. No other answer options contains less vowels, so therefore this is the correct answer.

Q25. A = Nigel

EXPLANATION = Mark can run faster than Jane (that makes Jane the slowest so far). Jane can run faster than Nigel (so that now puts Nigel as the slowest). Nigel is slower than Bill (that means Nigel is still the slowest). Bill runs faster than Mark (both of these are faster than Nigel). Therefore Nigel is the slowest.

VERBAL REASONING
(SECTION 5)

In each of the following questions, find the letters that best complete the series. The alphabet has been provided to assist you.

A B C D E F G H I J K L M N O P Q R S T U V W X Y Z

Question 1

DY EX FW GV HU [ ]

A – IT

B – JT

C – IS

D – IU

E – JS

Answer [   ]

Question 2

BA   CB   DC   ED   FE   [ ]

A – HF

B – GE

C – HE

D – FG

E – GF

Answer [   ]

Question 3

MN   LO   KP   JQ   IR   [ ]

A – HS

B – IS

C – IR

D – HR

E – HL

Answer

Question 4

Which one letter can be moved from the first word, to the second word, i
order to make two new words?

float   *range*

A	B	C	D
O	A	F	T

Question 5

Which one letter can be moved from the first word, to the second word, i
order to make two new words?

beret   *are*

A	B	C	D
B	E	R	T

Question 6

A word is hidden amongst the sentence. It has four letters and is hidden at the end of one word and beginning of the next word. What is the hidden word?

He was ignorant to the facts being handed to him.

Answer   sign

Question 7

A word is hidden amongst the sentence. It has four letters and is hidden at the end of one word and beginning of the next word. What is the hidden word?

During the football, you were lucky to score.

Answer

Question 8

A word is hidden amongst the sentence. It has four letters and is hidden at the end of one word and beginning of the next word. What is the hidden word?

They said they would come another time.

Answer   mean

Question 9

A word is hidden amongst the sentence. It has four letters and is hidden in one word and beginning of the next word. What is the hidden word?

The dog was frightened by the noise outside.

Answer

Question 10

If the code for CHORUS is EJQTWU, what does CNKGP mean?

A	B	C	D
Alien	Alley	Aleen	Alein

Question 11

If the code for FINE is GKQI, what does MGIX mean?

A	B	C	D
Heft	Left	Lets	Hest

Question 12

Which of the answer options has the most opposite meaning to – *innocent*?

A	B	C	D	E
Naïve	Virtuous	Malicious	Blameless	Chaste

Question 13

Which of the answer options has the most opposite meaning to – *gigantic*?

A	B	C	D	E
Colossal	Sized	Minuscule	Large	Average

Question 14

Which of the answer options has the most opposite meaning to – *serious*?

A	B	C	D	E
Severe	Important	Profound	Vital	Petty

Question 15

Which of the answer options has the most similar meaning to – *confident*?

A	B	C	D	E
Assertive	Insecure	Loud	Secret	Watchful

Question 16

Which of the answer options has the most similar meaning to – *faithful*?

A	B	C	D	E
Deceitful	Honest	Untrue	Biased	Devious

Question 17

Which word is the odd one out?

A	B	C	D	E
Lawnmower	Hose	Rake	Carpet	Shovel

Question 18

Which word is the odd one out?

A	B	C	D	E
Football	Wrestling	Table Tennis	Golf	Rugby

Question 19

Find the two words, one from each group, that come together to make a new word. (The word on the left always comes first in the new word).

(arm raft after)   **(jog chair old)**

Answer [   ]

Question 20

Find the two words, one from each group, that together make a new word. (The word on the left always comes first in the new word).

(at new be)   **(left side up)**

Answer [   ]

Question 21

Find the two words, one from each group, that together make a new word. (The word on the left always comes first in the new word).

(in knock round)   **(but out hind)**

Answer [   ]

Question 22

Find the two words, one from each group, that together make a new word. (The word on the left always comes first in the new word).

(cross hard angry)　　　　*(world word nail)*

Answer [　　　　　　　　　]

Question 23

Complete the following sentence.

She couldn't _____ any sweets, as her mother told her she _____ allowed.

A – have / was

B – eat / couldn't

C – choose / shouldn't

D – have / wasn't

E – throw / was

Answer [　　　　　　　　　]

Question 24

Complete the following sentence.

She looked _____ and _____ before crossing the road.

A – up / down
B – left / right
C – in front / behind
D – across / behind
E – over / beyond

Answer

Question 25

Which letter completes the following words?

BOO (?) NIGHT and **THIN (?) EEL**

A – D
B – K
C – L
D – M

Answer

ANSWERS TO SECTION 5

Q1. A = IT

EXPLANATION = the first letter in each group starts with *D*, then *E*, then *F*, *G*, *H*... and so the first letter of the next pattern needs to start with an *I*. The second letter of the group starts with *Y*, then *X*, then *W*, *V*, *U*... and so the next letter would need to be *T*. This gives you *IT*.

Q2. E = GF

EXPLANATION = the first letter in each group starts with *B*, then *C*, then *D*, *E*, *F*... and so the first letter of the next pattern needs to start with an *G*. The second letter of the group starts with *A*, then *B*, then *C*, *D*, *E*... and so the next letter would need to be *F*. This gives you *GF*.

Q3. A = HS

EXPLANATION = the first letter in each group starts with *M*, then *L*, then *K*, *J*, *I*... and so the first letter of the next pattern needs to start with an *H*. The second letter of the group starts with *N*, then *O*, then *P*, *Q*, *R*... and so the next letter would need to be *S*. This gives you *HS*.

Q4. A = O

EXPLANATION = if you removed the 'o' from 'float', you would get 'flat'. If you put the 'o' in the word 'range', you would get 'orange'.

Q5. C = R

EXPLANATION = if you removed the 'r' from 'beret', you would get 'beet'. If you put the 'r' in the word 'are', you would get 'rare'.

Q6. Sign

EXPLANATION = 'wa**s ign**orant'.

Q7. Ally

EXPLANATION = 'foot**ball, y**ou'

Q8. Mean

EXPLANATION = 'co**me an**other'.

Q9. Then

EXPLANATION = '**the n**oise'.

Q10. A = alien

EXPLANTION = the first word is coded by adding two letters of the alphabet from that letter. For example the letter 'c' in chorus' is coded 'e' (two letters up in the alphabet). So to work out what the code is representing, you need to work two letters backwards to find out the original word.

Q11. B = left

EXPLANATION = the code for the first letter in the word, is moving up the alphabet one space (f = g). The second letter is moving up two spaces (l = k). The third letter is moving up three spaces (n = q). The fourth letter is moving up four spaces (e = i). So to work out the original word in the next part of the sequence, you need to work backwards, so one space back, two spaces back and so forth.

Q12. C = malicious

EXPLANATION = 'innocent' has the most opposite meaning to 'malicious'.

Q13. C = minuscule

EXPLANATION = 'gigantic' has the most opposite meaning to 'minuscule'.

Q14. E = petty

EXPLANATION = 'serious' has the most opposite meaning to 'petty'.

Q15. A = assertive

EXPLANATION = 'confident' has the most similar meaning to 'assertive'.

Q16. B = honest

EXPLANATION = 'faithful' has the most similar meaning to 'honest'.

Q17. D = carpet

EXPLANATION = 'carpet' is the odd one out because all of the other words refer to items that can be found in the garden.

Q18. B = wrestling

EXPLANATION = 'wrestling' is the odd one out because all of the other words refer to sports that use a ball.

Q19. Armchair

EXPLANATION = you can put the word 'arm', with the word 'chair', to make the new word 'armchair'.

Q20. Beside

EXPLANATION = you can put the word 'be', with the word 'side', to make the new word 'beside'.

Q21. Knockout

EXPLANATION = you can put the word 'knock', with the word 'out', to make the new word 'knockout'.

Q22. Crossword

EXPLANATION = you can put the word 'cross', with the word 'word', to make the new word 'crossword'.

Q23. D = have / wasn't

EXPLANATION = *She couldn't **have** any sweets, as her mother told her she **wasn't** allowed.*

Q24. B = left / right

EXPLANATION = She looked **left** and **right** before crossing the road.

Q25. B = K

EXPLANATION = *book, knight, think* and *keel.*

ANSWERING YOUR QUESTIONS

You have now reached the end of your Kent Test booklet for Verbal Reasoning You should now feel confident enough to tackle any Verbal Reasoning question that you will encounter. Before you go, we recommend that you read through our final tips on how to answer the questions. You can use these tips in practice, and in your assessment.

Remember, for each exam in the Kent Test, you will be provided with a testing booklet and an answer booklet. These will be similar to the following:

- Maths and English Testing Booklet;
- Maths and English Answer Sheet;
- Reasoning Testing Booklet;
- Reasoning Answer Sheet.

You need to read the questions in the testing booklet and choose the correct answer, which you **MUST** then write on the answer sheet provided. When you take the Kent Test, only the answers written on the answer sheet will be marked. Any other written work or rough drafts on additional paper or in the testing booklet, will not be marked.

Make sure that at the start of your Kent Test, you take the time to read through the set of instructions on the front of your examination booklet. This will tell you everything you need to know regarding the Kent Test, including how to use the answer booklet and where to write your answers.

- Make sure that you mark your chosen answer to the corresponding question number. For example, if you answered question 5, make sure that you mark the answer to question 5!

- Any rough work, drafts or calculations should not be written on the answer sheet. Instead you should ask for extra sheets of paper or write them in your testing booklet. (Any additional paper or the testing booklet will not be marked!)

Example Answer Sheet

Here is a basic example marking sheet which gives you some indication of what you can expect in your assessment. For example, if you chose answer option 'D' as the correct answer for question 1 on the Verbal test, you would mark a line in pencil or pen, horizontally through the box (as shown).

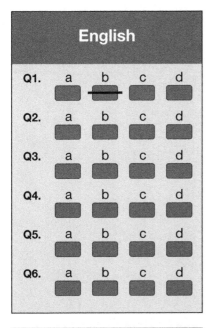

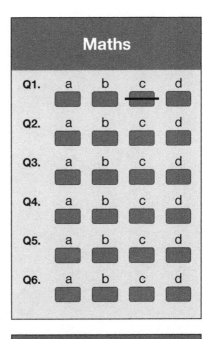

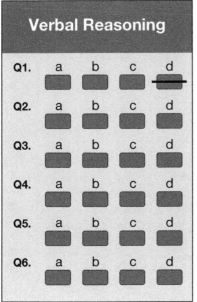

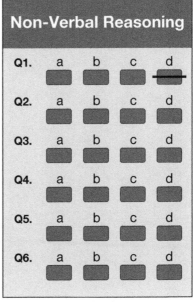

Good luck with your 11+ Kent Test, Verbal Reasoning. We wish you the very best of luck with all your future endeavours!

The how2become team

The How2Become Team

WANT MORE HELP WITH THE KENT TEST?

CHECK OUT OUR OTHER KENT TEST GUIDES:

How2Become have created other FANTASTIC guides to help you and your child learn all they need to pass the Kent Test.

There are 100s of practice questions within these guides all with detailed explanations. These guides also include expert insider tips and advice to help you or your child feel at ease on exam day.

FOR MORE INFORMATION ON OUR KENT TEST WORKBOOKS, PLEASE CHECK OUT THE FOLLOWING:

WWW.HOW2BECOME.COM

Get Access To
FREE
Educational Practice Papers
(KS2, 11+, KS3, GCSE)

www.MyEducationalTests.co.uk

Made in the USA
Las Vegas, NV
03 June 2022

49757537R00050